PICKERING & THORNTON-LE-DALE THEN & NOW

SUSAN McGILL & COLIN WATERS

The History Press

First published in 2012

The History Press
The Mill, Brimscombe Port
Stroud, Gloucestershire, GL5 2QG
www.thehistorypress.co.uk

ISBN 978 0 7524 6794 8

Typesetting and origination by The History Press
Manufacturing managed by Jellyfish Print Solutions Ltd
Printed in India.

CONTENTS

ACKNOWLEDGEMENTS

Though most of the old and all of the new photographs in this book are from the authors' collections, grateful thanks are due to everyone (including those who chose to remain anonymous) who provided additional images for copying, or supplementary historical information. Special thanks are extended to Mr Alwyn Dudley Smith of Thornton Dale Estate; the lady at the Fox and Rabbit Inn; the helpful staff at Wardill Brothers; Pickering Railway employees; Mrs G. Brown, for use of his scrapbook album; David Collins of Pickering; Pickering and District Conservative Club; the unnamed gardener at the former old mill in Thornton-le-Dale and the similarly unnamed postwoman who was delivering near the mill on the same day and who took time to give us helpful assistance. On a personal level, the authors would also like to thank the production team at History Press, especially Jessica Andrews, Project Editor, for her ever-friendly assistance during every stage of the production of this book.

ABOUT THE AUTHORS

Colin Waters is a writer, researcher and social historian and has contributed to radio, television, newspapers and national magazines. He was the founder and former director and president of Whitby Archives & Heritage Centre.

Susan McGill graduated with an honours degree in English literature and history and now works as a professional Internet researcher. She has a keen interest in the history of North Yorkshire, where she lives with her husband and two children.

INTRODUCTION

According to the Reverend George Young in a Yorkshire history book written in 1817, Pickering is the only place in this region that is mentioned in the fables of Geoffrey of Monmouth, who related that a castle was built here by an ancient British king named Perederus: '...long before the birth of Christ'. Many historians do believe the town was founded by Perederus, who lived around 270 BC and who it is said is buried on a peak 'on the brow of a hill called Rawcliff'. The town's name has been linked to a legend that the monarch lost his ring in the river and afterwards recovered it from a pike's stomach. Others believe that Pickering is a modern version of *pik-ing*, meaning 'a river meadow near the peak', whilst a third, more mundane, explanation says that Pickering is simply a corruption of 'pig-run', linking it firmly to the town's agricultural past.

When the sixteenth-century antiquary John Leland visited Pickering in the 1500s he described it as a large but not very compact town; no doubt at that time the old market place cross, which was described as being situated there in 1476, was still in place. It appears to have been dismantled some time before the mid-1800s and was replaced by another market cross on Smiddy Hill in 1912. Like all Yorkshire towns, the market place served as the cultural and business centre of the town and contained a group of butchers' premises known as the Shambles. Nearby, to the north, were the town pump and the village stocks where miscreants were punished, just as they were in the market place at Thornton-le-Dale where a set of stocks are still to be seen.

It is difficult to imagine, but until relatively modern times the roads around Pickering and Thornton-le-Dale were in a very rough state indeed, and it wasn't until 1759 that a turnpike road provided a reliable means for stagecoaches to reach the coast. Plans to build a canal between Pickering and Whitby in 1793 came to nothing, and residents had to wait until the opening of the Pickering to Whitby Railway to visit the seaside easily. The track was opened in 1836 amidst great celebration, including music from five bands positioned around the town and cannons being fired at intervals from the castle walls.

Today visitors are drawn here not only by Pickering and Thornton-le-Dale's numerous historical delights but also to explore the surrounding moorlands, satellite villages and other rural locations. Because of their close proximity, they offer a wide variety of opportunities for short drives, steam-train rides and pleasant walks to places such as the tiny ninth-century church of Ellerburn. Hidden away in an idyllic rural situation, it is only a short walk or drive from Thornton-le-Dale's market cross and provides yet another example of the often-missed secrets to be found waiting around every corner in this fascinating part of rural North Yorkshire.

SALTERSGATE

APPROACHING PICKERING VIA the A169, the historic Saltersgate Inn sits at the foot of the 'Devil's Elbow' on Saltersgate Bank (often misspelt Saltergate on modern maps and road signs). This inn, situated on the old Whitby to Pickering sea-salt merchants' route, was once an important coach stop between Pickering and Whitby. It is linked to a number of smuggling

stories including a legendary fire that supposedly never went out despite the passing of hundreds of years. The old photograph shows the inn at a time when a new road had just been laid to replace the old winding track (seen on the right of the photograph).

AS THIS MODERN photo of the 'Devil's Elbow' shows, the road has been further widened. The inn itself (seen in the distance with a blue roof) is at present in a dilapidated state. The substantial buildings shown to its right on the previous picture have vanished altogether, as has the old winding track, which is now covered with a plantation of trees. The building to be seen on the skyline is the 'pyramid' shaped radar installation at Fylingdales Ballistic Missile Early Warning Station. It replaced three 84ft-wide radomes, popularly known as 'golf balls', which were removed in the early 1990s.

SALTERSGATE INN

A CLOSER LOOK at the old inn in 1915 shows the old unsurfaced road and stepping stones (pannier-man's track) to its right. The road was barely used at that time and children can be seen relaxing near the old gate to the left. Inset is a picture of the legendary fire that was reputed to never have gone out. It burned local peat taken from the nearby moorlands. There has been speculation that the fireplace may have concealed the entrance to a priest hole where Catholic priests were hidden as they moved across the country during Britain's repression of Catholicism.

THE SAD STATE of this once attractive inn is a matter of concern to all who have visited it over the years. Before the new drink-driving laws, which were introduced in 1965, its bars were packed with customers from Pickering, Whitby and the surrounding villages. Today it appears that plans to refurbish it have come to a standstill, and despite being protected by security fencing, the dilapidated building has now attracted the attention of vandals. The fence is also being used to display advertising posters including those for The Alternative Living Fair Festival and the Whitby 1960s theme festival.

HOLE OF HORCUM

THE ROAD LEADING between Saltersgate and Pickering provides a fine view of the Hole of Horcum, a 400ft deep glacial depression in the picturesque moorlands north-east of the town. The working farm seen at the bottom of the steep decline was later abandoned, allowing nature to gradually reclaim the

fields, covering them with moorland heather and ferns. The massive depression, a glacial geological feature, is explained by a local legend that says it was caused by Wade, a Saxon giant, who scooped up a large handful of earth and threw it at his wife during a domestic argument.

THE AREA NOW serves as a popular centre for walkers from Pickering and beyond. The recent introduction of a parking charge at the formerly free North Yorkshire Moors National Park Authority car park (overlooking the Hole of Horcum) has not proved popular, particularly as it serves as an ideal starting point for these hikers. From here it is a short walk to Newton Dale Gorge where there are magnificent views of the steam trains from the North Yorkshire Moors steam railway. The railway has its terminals at Pickering and Grosmont, and has now extended its route to the seaside at Whitby.

THE FOX AND RABBIT BETWEEN PICKERING AND THORNTON-LE-DALE

THE FOX AND Rabbit, situated at the road junction just a short distance from both Pickering and Thornton-le-Dale, was once well known for its inn sign on a small post-mounted windmill that provided the inn's only electricity. The early photograph above may show the Allanson family. An entry in the *Malton Messenger* records a marriage on 10 December 1863 at Middleton parish church between Mr Thomas Allenson of the Fox and Rabbit Inn, and

Martha, the eldest daughter of Mr John Merry (yeoman) and the niece of the late Jonathan Merry of Lockton.

IT CAN BE seen from the modern photograph above that the Fox and Rabbit retains its original building, which may once have been High House Farm. A 'High House or Fox and Rabbit farm' is mentioned in an 1830 document as 'being near-unto Pickering'. The original building in the centre can be seen to have been extended, virtually tripling its size since the Victorian period. Where once stagecoaches and itinerant travellers on donkey and horseback served as its main customers, today the venue serves as a modern gastro pub, attracting regulars from nearby Pickering, Thornton-le-Dale and further afield.

THE WORKHOUSE

BOTH THORNTON-LE-DALE (1774) and Pickering (1776) are recorded as having poorhouses for those who could not support themselves. In 1838 the Poor Law Guardians brought an end to the custom of housing women and children at Thornton-le-Dale and males at Pickering and instead constructed a building to accommodate both groups on the Whitby road, at a cost of £1,550. The new poorhouse (shown on this map) accommodated 100 inmates. At that time males were

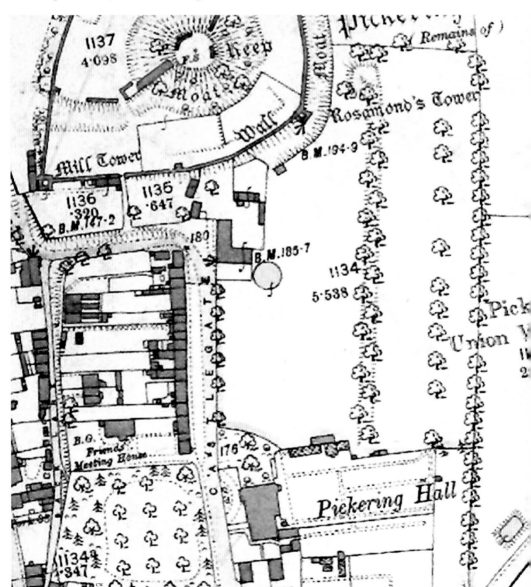

employed breaking stones for road works whilst the women unpicked 'oakum' rope fibres, which were sold for the sealing of ships' planks.

TODAY'S SCENE IS completely different. Gone are the imposing Victorian buildings, which had grown over the years to include a small punishment cell built in 1843, an infirmary in 1874 and a 'vagrant's ward' in 1878. It is recorded that in 1881 the workhouse master and matron were husband-and-wife team Francis and Mary Maul, who were both in their thirties. Francis was born at Birdsall, York; Mary was a local Pickering girl. The plot, situated only a few minutes walk from the town centre, is now the site of an old people's home.

CASTLEGATE/
BURGATE

CASTLEGATE GIVES ACCESS to the castle entrance, which is just out of shot to the left, in the distance behind the old thatched cottage, in the old postcard above. It forms the most northern end of Burgate. In 1868, the following was recorded:

> 'the Society of Friends has a meeting house, with burial ground, in Castlegate, where the Friends meet every third Sunday in the month. An adult first day (Sunday) school is held every week.'

The Quakers' building is still in existence with a nearby ancient *mort*, or set of stone steps, which were used for mounting horses and as a resting place for coffin bearers.

THE MODERN PHOTOGRAPH below shows the same scene today on Burgate (anciently, in 1438, spelt Burghgate). The single-storey thatched cottage in the old postcard has been replaced by a twin-storey modern dwelling. It can be seen that there have been some changes to the walls around the castle also, with the low-lying stone wall having been removed entirely. The footpaths have also been changed since the old photograph was taken, though the trees remain remarkably similar. A local directory tells us that in 1890 a local businessman, William Hill, a broom maker by trade, lived in one of the cottages in Burgate. Other residents to be found in Burgate in the same year include J.W. Simpson, the town's vaccination officer and registrar of births, marriages and deaths; F.W. Tyler, Inland Revenue officer; L. Beadle, dressmaker; J. Blench, vet; and M. Watson, basket maker.

THE CASTLE

PICKERING CASTLE IS seen here in an early photograph from the air together with a map dating from perhaps the 1940s. During the Civil War the castle was besieged by the parliamentary forces and was considerably damaged. From its walls the early inhabitants would have had a bird's eye view of the town. A Victorian description describes its situation as follows: '... on one side is a barren mountainous district, called Black, or Blake moor, which extends to a considerable distance, and furnishes materials for making brooms; on the river Costa, which rises at Kildhead... are several flour-mills.'

AFTER THE CIVIL War its walls were largely left to decay with stones being used for local building projects. A manorial court for all civil matters worth under forty shillings was held in one of the towers that had remained largely unscathed; the court was held on the second and third Mondays after Easter, and on the first and second Monday after Michaelmas. The twelfth-century chapel within the grounds has also been restored at various periods. This modern picture shows the Mill Tower, the others being Rosamund's Tower, Diate Hill Tower and the central Coleman tower, which was once used as the king's prison.

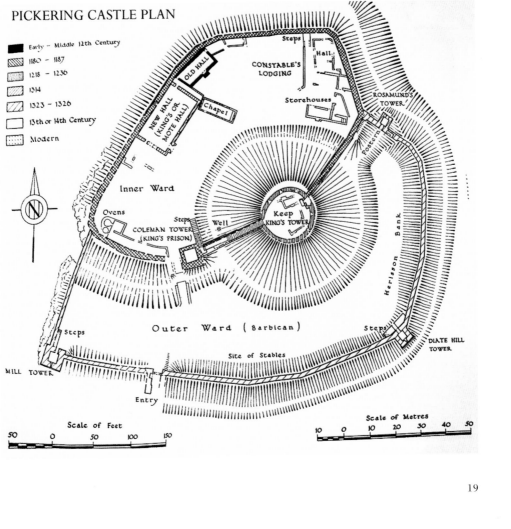

PICKERING CASTLE PLAN

Early – Middle 12th Century

1180 – 1187

1218 – 1236

1314

1323 – 1326

13th or 14th Century

Modern

Steps

CONSTABLE'S LODGING

Hall

OLD HALL

NEW HALL (KING'S OR MOTE HALL)

Chapel

Storehouses

ROSAMUND'S TOWER

Postern

N

Inner Ward

Ovens

COLEMAN TOWER (KING'S PRISON)

Steps

Well

Keep KING'S TOWER

Herisson Bank

Outer Ward (Barbican)

Steps

Steps

DIATE HILL TOWER

Site of Stables

MILL TOWER

Entry

Scale of Feet

50   0   50   100   150

Scale of Metres

10   0   10   20   30   40   50

THE GATEHOUSE

THE PICTURE OPPOSITE, taken at the castle gatehouse, shows two former Duchy of Lancaster officials taking part in the medieval 'riding t' fair' custom that died out in the late 1800s when the Pickering local board purchased toll rights from the Duchy. The Steward and tenants would ride from the castle to the market place on the date of the annual fair to declare the right to buy and sell '...horses, geldings, cattle, sheep, swine, and all sorts of merchandise' and to announce that any disputes that arose during the fair would be heard by the local pyepowder court.

TODAY THE GATEHOUSE serves as the tourist entrance to the castle, which is now administered by English Heritage, who advertise its historic attractions with a modern twist. They offer an exhibition, family fun books and attractions in the restored medieval chapel, the delights of the keep (known as the King's Room) and extensive views of North Yorkshire countryside. History lovers are pleased to find that other similar attractions are in close proximity, such as Helmsley Castle (12 miles), Scarborough Castle (15 miles), Whitby Abbey (18 miles), Clifford's Tower, York (23 miles), and Skipsea Castle (28 miles).

CASTLE MOUND

ORIGINALLY PICKERING CASTLE was built as a simple Norman motte-and-bailey construction consisting of a wooden castle mounted on top of a grassy mound that would have been surrounded by protective earth banks and ditches. The stone remains we see today date from the early thirteenth century, whilst the walls and towers date from the time of Edward II.

This picture, taken from a souvenir programme for the Pickering Pageant of 1910, features local residents at the foot of the mound enacting King John's arrival at the castle to present a charter to the nuns of Wykeham in 1201.

THE MODERN PICTURE shows the mound as it appears today with visitors who have just entered the area known as the Outer Ward or Barbican, with the remains of the keep and the Coleman Tower or King's Prison in front of them. A number of important prisoners are said to have been incarcerated in the castle including King Richard II. During a dispute between the Cholmleys and Hastings families – both of which claimed administration rights and fought bitter court battles in around 1499 – an unnamed prisoner was once released from the castle by a party using ladders under cover of darkness.

PICKERING PAGEANT

IN AUGUST 1910 when the pageant scene shown on the previous page was in the planning stage, rehearsals took place on a regular basis. The old photograph shows three of the main organisers after one of their evening rehearsals. Standing on the left is Mrs J. Kirk, one of two

MRS. KIRK.   MR. HUDSON.   REV.

"LEAVING THE REHEARS

JONES.

general secretaries, with Gilbert Hudson, the 'pageant master', alongside her. To their right is the Reverend D.E. Jones, vicar of Newton-upon-Rawcliffe, the 'music master'. Mr Hudson was a native of York and had a long record of organising similar pageants elsewhere. He was also skilled at writing music.

THIS PICTURE, TAKEN at the same spot, at the top of Burgate/Castlegate, shows the same building in the distance but with the wall in the old photograph having been completely demolished. Instead, a pleasant walkway has been constructed leading from the top of Burgate to the castle entrance between closely mowed lawns. The young tree behind Mr Hudson has been left in place and has now grown into a mature tree. It is interesting to see that bicycles feature in both pictures and that children can be seen in the background enjoying the safety of their off-road biking area.

HIGH MILL

THIS EARLY LETTERHEAD engraving dating from 1872 (below) is believed to be High Mill despite its heading, 'Pickering Steam Mills'. It is known that in the mid-1800s the mill was only a single-storey structure, later undergoing expansion both upwards and outwards. Though undoubtedly originally powered by water, the mill was later converted to steam and continued to produce flour from locally grown corn. In later years the mill owners manufactured animal feeds. Over the years the water wheels, mechanical parts and millstones were taken away, and in 1958 the mill ceased production, remaining unused from that time onwards.

HIGH MILL HOUSE is now under private ownership and the building is gradually being transformed from a derelict building into four-star holiday accommodation. Additional buildings have also been built on the former garage plot, stables and builders' yard. Over an eight-year period its new owners have fixed leaking roofs, replaced rotten woodwork and installed a central heating and hot-water system, luxuries which previous owners could not even have dreamed of. It is nice to see that one remnant of its distant past has been retained: the name of former owners 'W. Lumley and Sons, Agricultural Merchants'.

ERING STEAM MILLS.

April 1st 1872

CKERING. YORKSHIRE.

BRANT HILL

ONLY A STONE'S throw from High Mill is the long steep bank known as Brant Hill. This rather grainy old photo shows this ancient horse road consisting of a steep bank and steps connecting Park Street and Burgate as it was in around 1900. At the left of the picture, near the bottom of the bank, can be seen a water pump, and above the second boy, to the left, a roaming chicken. No one appears to know why the cottages to the right were nicknamed Wasp's Nest other than a

supposition that they may once have been swarming with large families.

THOUGH THE WATER pump is no more, Brant Hill looks much as it did in former times. Today it is used by tourists as a shortcut from the popular steam railway nearby to the ruins of Pickering Castle, which stand on the mound at the top of the town. In the modern picture, one small boy can be seen looking back. His clothing contrasts greatly with that worn by the children in the old picture. Today the houses are much smarter but still retain the essential historical quality of old Pickering when the word *brant* or *brent* meant a steep hill.

BRIDGE STREET

BRIDGE STREET CROSSES the river from Park Street to Potter Hill. The bridge is believed to be a successor to the 'Stanbrig' mentioned in 1476. Nearby stand old mill buildings now converted to modern premises. In the background, at the end of the street, can be seen the gates to the railway crossing, and on the left is Thomas Fletcher's shop with its large name sign and windows shaded with canvas blinds, indicating that they probably sold foodstuffs, though it may have been a general dealers as it is listed in the 1890 Pickering trades directory under the heading 'Miscellany of Trades'.

AS CAN BE seen from the modern view, the railway gates have now vanished and the line, which once crossed the road at that point, has disappeared for good. Fletcher's shop, though very much altered, is still in place and now sports modern blinds. On the right in both pictures can be seen the Rose public house. Its landlord in 1890 was William Britton. The pub is believed to have its origins in the 1600s and as such has become a listed building. Its structure is said to still contain remains of the original cruck timber framing.

WHITE SWAN

STANDING ALMOST AT the centre of the market place is the White Swan public house. The sketch opposite shows it as it was in 1922 when the street was devoid of traffic and the old shops on the opposite side of the road had not been given their modern frontages or large glass window panes. Just out of the picture (to the left) would have been the post office building. It too now houses modern shops and its former coach entrance leads to the modern flea market. In 1823 the postmaster was James Wilsthorp, and in 1840, presumably after his death, his wife Mrs Frances took over as postmistress.

THE MODERN PICTURE above shows the bottom end of the market place with the White Swan (blue sign) to the right. It is interesting to see that the bow front with its small paned windows is still in place, though the shops opposite have been distinctly modernised since the old sketch was made. In 1822 the White Swan was described as one of the two principal inns in the town, the other being the Black Swan. The White Swan's recorded landlords include Roger Kirby (1823); Francis Champion (1829); John Ellis (1834); Robert Bellwood (1840); and Jane and William Coverdale (1890). In 1890 William Berriman ran a regular carrier service from the White Swan to Cropton.

FLETCHER'S FORGE

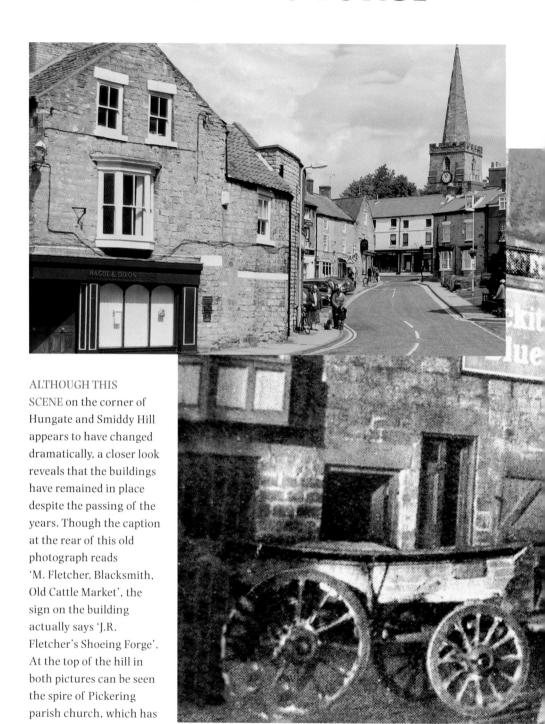

ALTHOUGH THIS SCENE on the corner of Hungate and Smiddy Hill appears to have changed dramatically, a closer look reveals that the buildings have remained in place despite the passing of the years. Though the caption at the rear of this old photograph reads 'M. Fletcher, Blacksmith, Old Cattle Market', the sign on the building actually says 'J.R. Fletcher's Shoeing Forge'. At the top of the hill in both pictures can be seen the spire of Pickering parish church, which has a treasure trove of medieval religious frescoes discovered in 1853 when whitewash was being removed during restoration work.

TODAY THE DISTRICT'S once numerous blacksmiths' premises have gone and the sounds of horses' hooves have been replaced by the noise of busy motor traffic. Much of it passes the bottom of this roadway, leading up to the market place from the nearby busy roundabout carrying traffic in four directions: to Whitby and Malton on the A169 and to Scarborough and Helmsley via the A170. At the top of the street all of the shops remain virtually the same as they were in the past, though Sawdon's shop sign, seen in the previous picture, has long since vanished.

CATTLE MARKET

THE OLD CATTLE market would once have been full of fences and pens in which to contain animals during the sale. It would also have been filled with farmers exchanging local gossip in the days before radio and television. This scene from an old postcard is not dated but appears to have been produced when the cattle market was already a distant memory. To the right is Hall Garth where, in 1871, John Jonas, the superintendent of police for Pickering Lythe Division, lived with his family at No.26. Jonas served with the North Riding Constabulary between 1856 and 1878.

IN THIS MODERN view of the Cattle Market area can be seen the Liberal Club, which celebrated its centenary in 2009. The building replaced the

former dwellings seen in the old picture, though those to its left remained. The demolished cottages were donated by a local councillor, John Frank, so that a new Liberal headquarters could be established in the town. The politician David Lloyd George visited the headquarters in 1931 during an election campaign. In 1986, David Steel, now Lord Steel, visited the headquarters in support of parliamentary candidate Elizabeth Shields. The central cross was erected in 1912.

BIRDGATE

THE TOP OF Smiddy Hill joins Birdgate, an ancient thoroughfare leading to the town's Market Place. This very old postcard shows the Black Swan Hotel (left) where in 1868 local magistrates once held court. Its landlord in 1890 was Ralph Loughorn. Other tradesmen in the street at that time included photographer Alfred Chapman; J. Dobson, joiner; Robert Fletcher, shopkeeper; John & Thomas Foster, drapers; Thomas Hodgson, fruiterer; William Jackson, plumber; Thomas Lightfoot, fishmonger; John Nellis, fruiterer; Christopher Sedman, hatter; Matthew Cross, butcher; and shoe makers and dealers Levi Massheder, Thomas Pamley and Joseph Wardell.

TODAY, THE BLACK Swan is still in existence but has lost its free-hanging name board. Other noticeable differences between the two pictures include the loss of the prominent Three Castles tobacco advertisement. This sign dates the old picture to after 1878 when the Wills tobacco company introduced 'Three Castles' and 'Gold Flake'. Other noticeable changes include the height of the tall chimney in the building on the right and the small window on the wall beneath it that has been filled in. In the distance distinct changes can also be seen to the buildings to the right of the picture.

ENTRANCE TO MARKET PLACE

THE END OF Birdgate marks the entrance into Pickering market place, the junction with Burgate and Willowgate (variously known in the fifteenth century as Wellesgate, Wolwardgate and Wollergate). The market must have been a busy place in earlier times with merchants selling a wide variety of goods. Early records show that the local court appointed a number of market

officials to regulate the quality of various goods on sale. These included two constables, two market searchers, two yarn tellers, two reeves, two ale tasters, two leather searchers, two pinders (to control stray animals) and two water searchers

THE OLD MARKET place must have been a very dark place in Victorian times when it was lit by gas. It is interesting to note that whilst a number of street lights line both sides of the road in the modern photograph, the old postcard shows only a single lamp stand. It would seem that gas street lighting came to Pickering with the railways when a railway gas works was built to light the station as well as the streets of the town. A private gas works later took over production and the railway gas works were decommissioned in 1892.

PARISH CHURCH

CLOSE TO THE point shown in the previous picture are a set of steps leading to Pickering parish church. The site has been used as a place of worship since Saxon times, and stonework, including part of a Saxon cross, can be found in or near the present structure. The bowl of the font is also believed to date from Saxon times. The present church is medieval, with additions having been made to its structure between the twelfth and sixteenth centuries. This old postcard shows the church when its grounds were virtually devoid of trees or bushes.

TODAY IT IS almost impossible to take a photograph of the complete church due to the trees and bushes surrounding it. This modern photograph shows that many of the early gravestones

and table type tombs pictured in the earlier photo have vanished. Some of them have disappeared due to damage and wear or were taken away when weathered stones collapsed or became unreadable. Others have been simply buried beneath undergrowth. Ryedale Family History group have uncovered a number of these in order to read their inscriptions and have now produced a CD containing digital photographs of every remaining stone.

THE TOWER

THIS PICTURE, SHOWING repairs to the tower, probably dates from 1877 when the church was thoroughly restored at a cost of over £8,000. Finance was obtained through public subscriptions with additional funds for the chancel being defrayed from the Ecclesiastical Commissioners' tithes income. Using great skill the workers removed the old tower foundations and substituted them with a new structure. Men can be seen precariously balancing on a swinging beam above their colleagues below. Other workers are stood on two ladders leaning against the tower, whilst a man in a top hat, probably the foreman, stands bottom left.

THE MAGNIFICENT CHURCH tower today stands firmer than ever and is a tribute to the Victorian workers who restored it with the most basic of constructional tools that probably differed very little from those used to build the church in ancient times. During the restoration, a number of very early artefacts were unearthed, confirming that a place of worship had stood on this same site since at least Saxon times. Restoration of the church also took place between 1190 and 1220, during which period the tower was constructed. The spire was added some time after the beginning of the fourteenth century.

FRESCOES

WITHOUT DOUBT, PICKERING parish church is best known for its interior walls, which are decorated with rare medieval frescoes of the sort that would have covered the walls of all English churches prior to the Puritan suppression of all religious 'ostentation'. Because of the technical limitations of the time, this old black and white postcard failed to do justice to the paintings, which were discovered in 1853 when the coloured figures were uncovered during cleaning. It is said that the vicar at the time insisted that the 'idolatry remnants of Papism' should be immediately obliterated with a fresh coat of whitewash.

LUCKILY PARISHIONERS AND clergymen of a later date were more open-minded. They set out to uncover the frescoes once more and discovered yet more illustrations on the church walls. This modern photograph shows the same scene, illustrating the life of St Catherine of Alexandria who became popular at the time of the crusades. Her voice was said to be one of those heard by Joan of Arc. She also became a prominent saint in the lives of the Knights Templar and patron saint of a whole spectrum of other sections of the community including virgins, students, philosophers, millers, wheelwrights and teachers.

HEROD'S FEAST

THIS BLACK AND white depiction of part of the church frescoes depicts the story of the martyrdom of John the Baptist and Herod's feast. The rest of the story, not depicted, tells the rest of the biblical story including John rebuking the king for his unlawful marriage and Salome's dance. It continues with a depiction of Salome holding a plate as John is beheaded and finally shows his head on a dinner plate, as can be seen in this picture. These cartoon-like stories were popular in English churches at a time when few could read or write.

HERE WE SEE the same scene (to the left of the picture) today in full colour. To the right is another 'comic strip' style depiction of the martyrdom of St Edmund, the king of East Anglia, who died on 20 November 840 AD. Though in reality he is believed to have died in battle against Viking invaders, popular and church culture perpetrated the story that he was martyred because he refused to renounce his Christian faith. No record appears to exist regarding the identity of the artists who painted these rare and historic valuable artefacts.

EFFIGIES

HERE WE SEE an old postcard showing the full interior of the church, though again the fact that it was in black and white doesn't do it justice. Today the scene is very little changed. Below the end of

Pickering Church.

the final arch on the left-hand side is a recumbent figure of a knight with his legs crossed, symbolising that the man served in Jerusalem as a crusader. In a side chapel opposite are a pair of similar

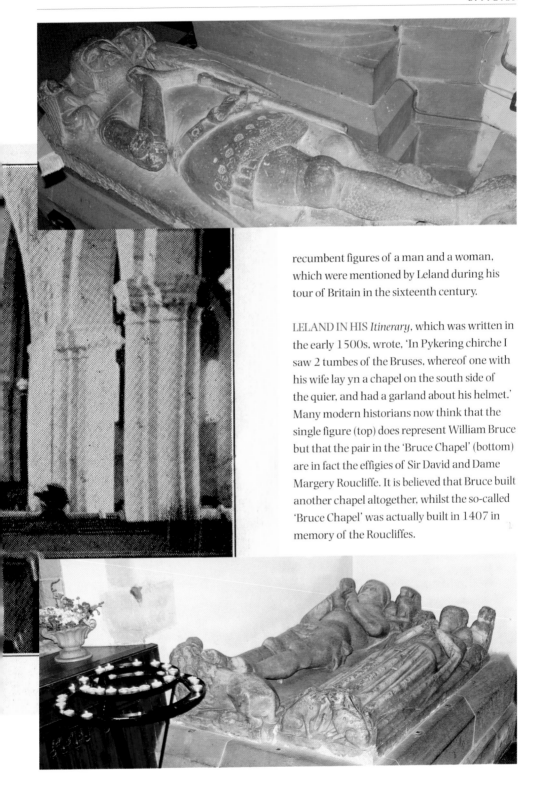

recumbent figures of a man and a woman, which were mentioned by Leland during his tour of Britain in the sixteenth century.

LELAND IN HIS *Itinerary*, which was written in the early 1500s, wrote, 'In Pykering chirche I saw 2 tumbes of the Bruses, whereof one with his wife lay yn a chapel on the south side of the quier, and had a garland about his helmet.' Many modern historians now think that the single figure (top) does represent William Bruce but that the pair in the 'Bruce Chapel' (bottom) are in fact the effigies of Sir David and Dame Margery Roucliffe. It is believed that Bruce built another chapel altogether, whilst the so-called 'Bruce Chapel' was actually built in 1407 in memory of the Rouclifles.

ROBERT KING

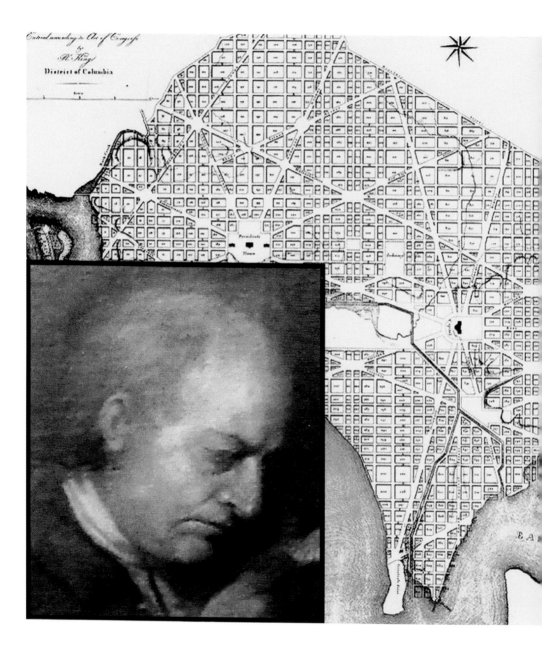

TUCKED AWAY IN a darkened corner of the church is a pillar upon which is hung a small portrait of one of Pickering's famous residents, Robert King. Robert, a surveyor, and his son Nicholas were instrumental in laying out the streets of Washington DC. Nicholas was Pickering born and bred and was christened in the parish church. He was later trained as a surveyor by his father before emigrating to America in 1794. He became Washington's official surveyor in 1796 and died in 1812. Nicholas was followed to America by his family, and in 1797 Robert also became Washington's surveyor.

Near the altar is a memorial to the King family, which reads:

In memory of Mary King [née Clark] who departed this life November 26th 1780 aged 36 years, and of Nicholas her eldest son, Surveyor of the city of Washington where he died May 31st 1812 aged 40 years. Also of Robert King her husband, who died December 2nd 1817 having been five years surveyor of the above city aged 77 years...

ROBERT RETURNED TO England and is buried at the foot of the church steps. The other King children were Robert (b. 17 March 1775) and Jane (b. 17 October 1780).

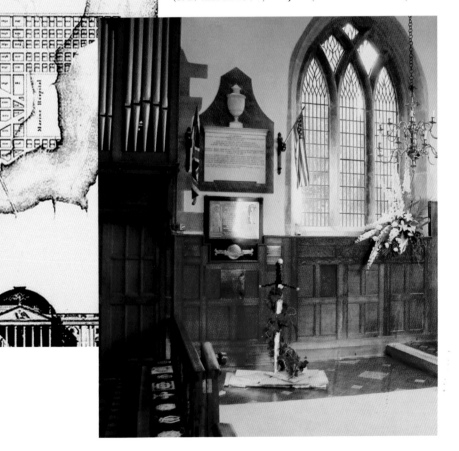

MARKET PLACE (TOP)

ONLY A STONE'S throw from the parish church is the town's market place. It was much more tranquil in the days before motor traffic, allowing children to sit in the middle of the road. Barrels and boxes can also be seen placed randomly along the street. The sign above the door of the White Swan appears to give the landlord's name as Herbert Hunt. No full list of previous landlords appears to exist but Roger Kirby owned the

pub in 1823, Francis Champion in 1829, John Ellis in 1834, Robert Bellwood in 1840 and J. and W. Coverdale in 1890.

TODAY'S SCENE IS much less tranquil. In former days the Shambles, or butchers' quarter, stood here and animals were once slaughtered on the premises. The shambles closed in 1857. Old records tell us that a market cross stood here in 1476 and a set of stocks stood nearby for the punishing of minor offenders. Fairs took place annually on the Mondays preceding 14 February, 13 May, 22 November, and the 25 September. The present market cross stands in Smiddy Hill and was erected in 1912 and commemorates the reign of Edward VII and the coronation of George V.

BREWERY BUILDING

THE SCARBOROUGH AND Whitby Breweries branch headquarters once stood in a prominent position at the top of the market place (No.16). As this picture (supplied by Pickering

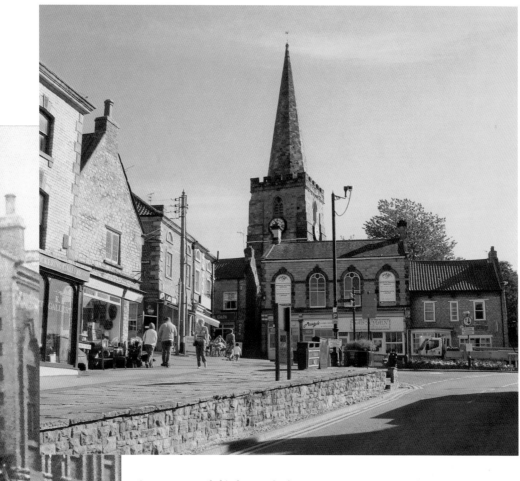

Conservative Club) shows, the business also acted as a wholesale merchant for the sale of cigars, tobacco and non-alcoholic drinks. The company also had similar premises at Westborough; Scarborough, where they had a bottling plant in North Street; 'The Vines', Malton; and Nos 1 and 3 Marine Parade, Whitby, where they had a shop at No. 25 Skinner Street. The brewery's trademark logo was an archer's target. A number of public houses were owned by the brewery throughout North Yorkshire, selling its own 'Chrysalis' brand ale.

THE BREWERY, KNOWN locally as 'the Vaults', was demolished in the late 1800s. It had been built on the site of earlier butchers' premises known as The Shambles, which were themselves demolished in 1857. The pavement to the left has now been raised and the buildings, which were situated behind the old vaults, can now be seen in full. It will be noticed that there has been a subtle change to the buildings on the left-hand side of the old picture where, unusually, a woman, not a man, appears to be clad in painter's overalls, climbing a ladder.

CENTRAL CAFÉ

THE CENTRAL CAFÉ was a popular meeting place in the days when this old picture was taken, presumably for an advertising postcard. It was evidently famous for its jam scones and Christmas gingerbread. The premises stood a little way down the street from the old post office's market place premises and on the same side. Though it is uncertain, this may be the same premises owned in 1823 by George Champley, a baker by trade. He was also listed as a baker and flour dealer in Pigot's 1829 Trade Directory. In 1834 the same business was being run by Susannah Champley.

IT IS SAID that the town crier would stand outside of the shops around the Central Café area to make his proclamations in a loud droning voice until around 1880, ringing a small medieval handbell that came from the castle. The bell was given to the British Museum where presumably it is still to be seen. The bell is engraved with a crucifix and the figures of St George and the Dragon, the Virgin and Child, and St John the Baptist, and an inscription on the bell reads 'Vilyame Stokeslai' (William of Stokesley). Today the old café is now a shop selling fishing tackle, anglers' supplies and outdoor wear.

CONSERVATIVE CLUB

EARLY CAMERAS WERE not quick enough to prevent the blurring of many of the people in this bustling picture of the opening of the Conservative Club's headquarters at No. 40 Market Street. (The Conservative Club supplied this excellent photograph.) Nevertheless, some people remained stationery enough to be recognisable, though sadly their names are not given. The building

f Conservative Club and Public Hall, Pi... Oct ...ns. Ro2.

was originally the palatial home of a prosperous gentleman, the Whitby whaling ship owner Nicholas Piper. One of his ships, the 251-ton *Henrietta*, was recorded in 1771 as being 89ft 9in long and 25ft 8in in breadth. It was built in 1764.

THE ORIGINAL BUILDING, which is now split in half, also houses Barclays Bank premises (to its left). Even so, the large three-storey building is an impressive piece of architecture and still retains its original bow topped windows and inside period layout. It also retains traditional cast-iron railings, as can be seen in the older picture. The club's opening took place on 24 October 1913. Few could have realised at that time that within less than a year, on 4 August 1914, the excitement of the opening would have been long forgotten, and that many of the town's young men would have been lost to enemy action in the First World War.

RAILWAY SIDINGS

AT THE FOOT of Market Street would have once been the crossing gates leading to Bridge Street. This old picture shows the railway line and sidings from the distant fields. The tower of the parish church can just be seen to the right of the picture, though the castle is missing from the view, being just out of shot to the left. At that time the trucks in the railway sidings were all goods trucks, showing that Pickering was a key part of the Whitby to York railway network following its absorption into the York and North Midland Railway in 1845.

THE SIDINGS TODAY
contain only passenger
carriages, as can be seen here
at the crossing near High
Mill. The wide path in the
foreground leads to another
narrower footpath along the
riverside, eventually opening
out into the fields shown
in the previous picture.
The steam trains that now
run along this route give
an insight into what travel
would have been like in the
days of steam, though an
even older railway system
preceded steam. The Whitby
and Pickering Railway
was one of Yorkshire's
first railways. It opened
in 1836 as a single-track
horse-drawn railway.

63

THE RAILWAY

ON THIS OLD engraving of the original horse-drawn railway between Whitby and Pickering we see passengers who have apparently missed the train shouting for it to stop at one of the mid-way stations. Though the line appears flat at this point, the engineer George Stephenson had to overcome much more difficult terrain along the route, including a steep slope from Beckhole to Goathland where a steep 1 in 15 incline was overcome using a strong rope to pull the carriages upwards. Bogs and marshland also posed a problem, which Stephenson overcame using woven hurdles and brushwood strengthened with clay.

THOUSANDS OF VISITORS annually flock to Pickering each year to experience travel on a steam locomotive. This picture shows the steam-train terminus at Pickering Station (though originally the line would have gone on to Malton and York). This particular locomotive is the *George Stephenson*, named after the engineer who was responsible for the opening of the original track between Pickering and Whitby. It was named by William Whitelaw MP at Shildon in 1975 to commemorate the 150th anniversary of the Stockton and Darlington Railway. It is kept in pristine condition by the North York Moors Historical Railway Trust Ltd.

EASTGATE

WE TAKE A final look at Pickering through an old postcard showing Eastgate, the road leading out of the town towards Thornton-le-Dale, *c.*1900. Among the premises pictured are the shops of Maurice Windlass, a rag-and-bone dealer who made and sold besom brooms. Next door (to the right) can be seen T.W. Hebden's premises where besom brooms were also manufactured from local heather, and where marine goods were sold. Until the late 1800s broom-making was a major craft industry in the town. Broom-makers in 1890 included Windlass; Hebden; James Hill (Eastgate); and William Hill (Burgate).

EASTGATE

THE SAME GROUP of buildings can be seen to the left in this modern photograph looking along Eastgate. It is interesting to note the height that the newly planted trees shown in the old postcard have achieved in just over 100 years and the 'street furniture' that has taken the place of the bare pavements of previous years, such as the notice board, flower-bedecked lamp post and bus stop. Interestingly, the bus stop on the opposite side of the road stands in front of a flat-fronted modern building that once served as the local bus depot.

THORNTON DALE

THE ROAD FROM Eastgate, Pickering, leads directly to the centre of Thornton-le-Dale with its market cross and stocks. In this old photograph we can see some distinctly dated motor vehicles. Though those parked to the left seem to be from the 1940s, the two on the right appear to belong to the early 1960s, giving no clue as to the date of the photograph. An old North Yorkshire County Council finger post, painted in the regulation black and white striped livery,

shows the distances to nearby towns. The black square sign behind it is the local bus stop.

TODAY THE SCENE is little changed from that in the previous pictures, though the large truck parked to the left of the cross is distinctly modern. Noticeable changes include the vanished North Yorkshire County Council road sign and the modern bus shelter that has taken the place of the wooden sign. The market cross sits at the crossroads of Thornton-le-Dale, with one road leading to Pickering and Malton, a second, to Scarborough, a third, to Whitby and (as the sign indicates) yet another along Maltongate, leading to Malton via another route.

MARKET CROSS

THIS EVEN OLDER scene pictured on a Victorian postcard at the same point is meant to illustrate the cross and stocks but is perhaps more interesting because of the old vehicle, its occupants and the children standing on the steps of the cross. The picture has an ethereal quality, and though obviously only meant to be a snapshot of local residents, it has a slightly sinister look that could easily be used on a modern street poster to illustrate a contemporary 'spooky' film. The vehicle has the registration number SN 20 and appears to be an early type of Morris convertible.

THORNTON DALE CROSS & STOCKS

THE OLD MARKET cross is a fine example of a 'stock' cross, meaning that it is in the form of a post with a rounded top rather than an actual cross. It is said that this style of cross has an ancient

history pre-dating religious crosses. The style actually gives its name to the wooden stocks nearby, rather than the other way round. Thornton-le-Dale's wooden stocks are not original but have been faithfully copied from those that once stood on the same site. A statute of 1405 ordered that every manor should provide stocks for the punishment of offenders.

CROSS ROADS

THE SCENE CAPTURED on this old postcard is photographed (probably sometime in the 1940s) from a point just down Maltongate, looking towards the crossroads. The market cross is just out of sight under the trees that can be seen on the right, beyond the children on the bridge. The attractive babbling stream runs throughout Thornton-le-Dale, giving the village a special character that is hard to duplicate elsewhere. Though there are new houses to be found here, they are carefully placed so as not to interfere with the town's historic arrangement: it contains around seventy listed buildings.

THE MODERN SCENE, taken around sixty years later, shows that Thornton-le-Dale is a timeless place. The railings surrounding the stream have not altered at all and even the porch of the house to be seen on the right is still in existence. Only the type and amount of road transport has changed. Maltongate is far from a busy highway and provides a pleasant route for walkers who feel the need to wander. The town's show field will also be found here, where events such as the annual show are a high point in the annual calendar for local residents.

THATCHED COTTAGE

ONE OF THORNTON-LE-DALE'S most famous
must-see sites is known by one and all as the Thatched
Cottage. This picturesque building with the stream
meandering close by has appeared on chocolate
boxes, postcards, calendars, paintings, tapestry kits,
jigsaws and countless films and photographs around
the world. The reason is not hard to see, because
whether captured in sepia, as on this old postcard,
or in full colour, its captivating beauty is undeniable.
The stream, known as Dalby Beck or Thornton Beck,
originates in nearby Dalby Forest which itself attracts
thousands of visitors each year.

THIS COLOURED PICTURE of the same scene, taken
from a wider angle, shows just how beautiful the
cottage appears as you approach it on the footpath
adjacent to the tree-lined beck (beck was the Viking
settlers' word for stream). The footpath is accessed from
what is traditionally called the Stone Bridge leading
towards the A170 Scarborough Road. Scenes such as
this show just why the area has become so popular and
why Thornton-le-Dale village, though fast becoming
a small town, still deserves its reputation as the most
attractive village in North Yorkshire.

STONE BRIDGE

THOUGH HAVING STOOD here for
generations, many locals are unaware
of the name Stone Bridge: indeed on this
old postcard it is written as one word,
'Stonebridge'. It crosses the stream
that runs through Thornton-le-Dale,
and carries the road from the town
centre to the church (which can
be seen in the background) and on
towards Scarborough. For such a small
geographical area it seems to have a
number of varying names. Some old
postcards refer to the same scene as
Stone Bridge Cascade, presumably a
reference to the stream below it, and
others to Bridge Foot.

THE SAME SCENE today is remarkably similar, though trees now obscure the view of All Saints' church, which could once be seen before crossing the bridge. To the left is the entrance to Brook Lane, whilst the small gap in the wall (centre left) leads to the riverside footpath, which in turn leads to the thatched cottage mentioned earlier. It also leads to Priestmans Lane, at the end of which is located Thornton Mill. To the right of the picture can be seen a small sign advertising The Hall residential home, a palatial building that was once a gentleman's residence and later a hotel.

THE HALL

THE OLD HALL, which dates from the 1600s, and the bridge itself can be seen below from a different angle on the footpath walk that runs alongside of the stream. At the left of the bridge is a stone-covered ramp where in days gone by farm animals, which were driven along the main road, could be led down to drink from the stream. At the time the old photograph was taken, the Hall had

not been extended – as can be seen from the extensive tree-filled gardens stretching in the direction of Thornton-le-Dale.

THE HALL TODAY has been extended, as can be seen from the buildings to the right of the main building in the modern photograph above. Despite this growth, the luxurious residential home still has extensive gardens and rightly claims to be a home from home rather than just an old people's home. The building still boasts extensive and well laid out gardens and has been restored to its former glory with chandeliers, plaster friezes, luxurious furnishings and a high-class restaurant in the charge of a high-class chef. Attached is the Hall Inn, which is open to residents and visitors alike.

THORNTON HALL

THOUGH THORNTON HALL is little changed from when this old photograph was taken, it has been considerably altered since it was first built around 1669 when the manor was purchased by John Hill, a retired silk merchant. The building remained in the possession of the Hill family until relatively modern times. It was occupied by Richard Johnson Hill, who died in 1793, and later by his son Richard in 1855. Richard's son, the Revd John Richard Hill, succeeded him in 1897, followed by his own son Richard. The next generation took over in 1906 when Capt. Richard Hill, JP, occupied it.

IT IS THOUGHT that the building was raised in height in the 1700s at a time when it probably had a whitewashed exterior. The hall today retains a dignified appearance, enhanced by the growth of red foliage on its outside walls. As can be seen when comparing the two pictures, the main doorway has been moved, though little else has changed. Today the coach drive is used as a modern car park for visitors to the Hall Inn, which serves everything from pub meals to à la carte food. It also hosts a range of specialised evening events.

BECK HALL

AT THE END of the footpath
leading past the thatched cottage
is a small footbridge that links it to
Priestman's Lane. Beck Hall, the
house in the photograph, dates to
1830, with late nineteenth-century
extensions. Priestmans Lane
appears to take its name from the
Priestman family who lived in Beck
Hall, which is now a Grade II listed
building. Official records of the
Priestman family are to be found in
the first records of Thornton-le-Dale
parish church. During the 1500s
and 1600s the name was spelt
Prestman and changed to the
present spelling early in the 1700s.

THIS MODERN SCENE shows Beck Hall and Priestmans Lane leading to Thornton Mill. In former times, layers of ivy covered the building and large trees swept down almost to the road surface, but the modern picture reflects a much tidier scene. One small difference between the two pictures is the change in the number of skylight windows on the roof. Otherwise the scene is largely unchanged from when the Priestman family lived there. Incidentally, the Priestmans were connected by descent to William Rowntree of the famous chocolate company in York. Arnold Rowntree bought Brook House on Priestmans Lane in 1939.

THORNTON MILL

THIS DELIGHTFUL PICTURE taken at Thornton Mill on Priestmans Lane shows an unnamed Victorian lady (and presumably her daughter) close to the small ford that crossed the road at that time. Hardly noticeable is another lady sitting below the hedge on the left almost in a meditating position. This building was originally a flour mill but later went on to produce animal feeds and has now been converted to flats. There were previously a number of other mills operating in the

THORNTON DALE - MILL.

Thornton and nearby Ellerburn, including fulling mills that processed cloth, a paper mill and others producing flour.

THE BRIDGE SEEN in the old picture is still in position, though the road has been lifted above the small stream so that a bridged area covers the former small ford. The mill buildings, which have been rebuilt in parts, are now surrounded by hedges. The road seen in both photographs circles round to the left, passing the local bowling club and eventually reaching the junction to Ellerburn before returning to the market cross area of Thornton-le-Dale and the crossroads leading to Pickering, Scarborough, Whitby and the roadway along Maltongate.

MALTONGATE

THE OLD POSTCARD below features the stream at Maltongate (looking towards
Thornton-le-Dale) in former times when things were quieter and the noise of traffic consisted
only of horses' hooves and the trundle of cart wheels. This postcard is undated, but the man
wearing a straw hat is a clue to the era: straw hats were very fashionable from before the First
World War to the 1920s. To the right, ducks and geese paddle in the stream near a shallow ford
leading to a farm gate, which, like the nearby railings, appears to be newly painted.

MALTONGATE, THORNTON

ALE. 257.

TODAY, THOUGH NOT very busy, cars have still spoilt the former tranquillity of the road. The owner of the horse and cart in the previous picture could never have imagined the amount of traffic that would pass down Maltongate in future years, or the modern problem of their drivers finding a place to park. The ford on the right where the ducks and geese were wallowing has now been covered with a small road bridge complete with its own railings (right) and the sparse vegetation of previous years has grown to provide the greenery along the beck side that we see today.

ALL SAINTS' CHURCH

ALL SAINTS' CHURCH stands on an imposing hill on the A170 leading towards Scarborough. When this rather indistinct photograph was taken the road was unsurfaced. The church stands on a distinctive raised mound and is believed to have replaced an earlier chapel some time in the fourteenth century. The tower and other additions were added in the fifteenth century. A major refurbishment took place between 1865 and 1866 when all of the windows were renewed, and a porch was added in 1900. Parliamentary troops, who left sword and pistol marks on the pillars, were billeted in the church during the Civil War.

THE PAVEMENT IS slightly narrower today and
the trees have grown to partially obliterate the
sight of the church, but the scene is largely
unchanged and would still be recognised today
by the boys in the old picture. On the right,
the old buildings have been converted to a
large warehouse selling antiques. The inside
of the church is quite interesting. Memorials
include one for Lady Beatrice Hastings, a former
supporter of the church, whose effigy lies in
the sanctuary. Sir Richard Cholmley, 'the Great
Black Knight of the North', who died in 1583, is
buried in the chancel. Sir Richard came from a
long line of distinguished family members who
were descended from the Cholmondleys, barons
of Malpas in Cheshire. He was a valiant soldier
who received his honour of knighthood in Leith
in 1544, and his family had control of many
distinguished Yorkshire properties including
Whitby Abbey following its dissolution.

HIGH
STREET

HIGH STREET, STRETCHING along
the A170 towards Scarborough above
the churchyard, is literally the highest
part of the village. Lined with houses
on both sides, there is no sign of the
normally ever-present stream found
in other parts of Thornton-le-Dale.
This old sketch is undated but quite
old, as the road is not surfaced and
there is no sign of traffic, either horse
drawn or vehicular. Just beyond the
first house on the right can be seen
the entrance to Rectory Lane, whilst
to the left is the narrow lane leading
up behind the church graveyard.

THE MODERN HIGH Street, like
many of the highways and byways

in Thornton-le-Dale, appears timeless and unchanged, apart from the modern surfacing of the road, which has slightly lowered the height of the path on the right. One noticeable difference is the roof on the building just beyond the entrance to Rectory Lane. Whilst in the old sketch it was thatched, today is has a roof of modern tiles. Beyond the houses which stretch on both sides of the road for some distance, the road opens out into countryside.

THE BLACK HOLE

DESPITE ITS SMALL size and rural location, the Thornton-le-Dale of old still must have had its law breakers (hence the village stocks). Though now largely undocumented, it also had its own village gaol situated on the road to Ellerburn church. This old sketch of the 'Black Hole' shows how it looked, possibly around 1910, long after the windowless lock-up ceased to be in use. Evidently, the last person to be incarcerated in the 'Black Hole' during the 1800s was a woman named Birdsall, who was released by four angry village men who broke down the door to set her free.

TODAY THE BLACK Hole is no more. The only sign of it appears as a slight indent surrounded by flowers in a private garden wall where the tiny doorway used to be. The Birdsalls were evidently no strangers to law breaking in ancient times: church visitation accounts for 1590 record the punishment of 'John Shaw [of Ellerburn] for fornication with Elizabeth Birdsall of the parish of Thorneton [le Dale]' and in 1619 Thomas and Luke Birdsall (weavers) of Thornton-le-Dale found themselves before Thirsk quarter sessions accused by the Puritan authorities of playing 'musical interludes' at New Malton and elsewhere.

ELLERBURN CHURCH

IT SEEMS FITTING to end this tour of Pickering and Thornton-le-Dale with a picture of one of the areas little-known secrets. This thousand-year-old church, shown here on a Victorian postcard, is in the hamlet of Ellerburn, just a stone's throw from Thornton-le-Dale. It can be easily reached on foot or by driving along a country track. Though tiny, it is considered the 'mother' church of the whole district because its earliest parts date back to the ninth century. During restoration work in the early 1900s, foundations of an even older religious building were discovered.

THIS ENIGMATIC 'PARISH' church of Ellerburn, which is dedicated to St Hilda, stands literally in a field and close to Thornton-le-Dale and the main road leading from it, yet its situation is so hidden from view that many come across it by accident. Those that do are enchanted by the peace and quiet of its location. Interestingly, according to a guide from the 1800s, ecclesiastically, Ellerburn does not actually exist at all. It states that 'Ellerburn Parish Church serves Wilton and Farmanby, nearly one mile hence. Though there is a parish of Ellerburn no actual village of the name of Ellerburn exists.'

Other titles published by The History Press

Haunted Yorkshire Dales

SUMMER STREVENS

Discover the darker side of the Dales with this terrifying collection of true-life tales from across the region. Featuring chapters on ecclesiastic ectoplasms, ghostly creatures, ladies in black and star-crossed spooks, this book is guaranteed to make your blood run cold. Drawing on historical and contemporary sources and containing many tales which have never before been published, *Haunted Yorkshire Dales* will delight everyone interested in the paranormal.

978 0 7524 5887 8

The Little Book of Yorkshire

GEOFFREY HOWSE

A fascinating, fact-packed compendium of the sort of information which no one will want to be without. The county's most eccentric inhabitants, famous sons and daughters, royal connections and literally hundreds of intriguing facts about Yorkshire's landscape, cities, towns and villages come together to make one handy, pocket-sized treasure trove of trivia. A remarkably engaging little book, this is essential reading for visitors and locals alike.

978 0 7524 5773 4

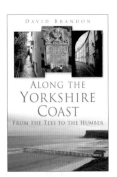

Along the Yorkshire Coast: From the Tees to the Humber

DAVID BRANDON

This book is a unique record of a journey along the beautiful and often dramatic Yorkshire coastline, tracing the region's diverse industry, the history of its settlements, seaside resorts and fishing quays, and reflecting upon the different uses to which man has put the resources where sea and land meet.With a blend of photographs, fact, folklore and social history, David Brandon offers a fascinating and evocative look at the county's local history, and should capture the imagination of anyone who knows the places that are featured.

978 0 7524 5732 1

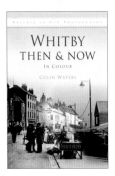

Whitby Then & Now

COLIN WATERS

In this fascinating volume, social historian Colin Waters has carefully selected a wide variety of captivating archive images, ranging from scenes of old narrow streets and local people to nostalgic harbour views and the town's majestic abbey. Each old picture is complimented with a modern colour photograph and a detailed caption, providing fascinating insights into the history of this charming town. Essential reading for all lovers of nostalgia and a welcome addition to the bookshelf of every lover of Whitby and its historic past.

978 0 7524 6315 5

Visit our website and discover thousands of other History Press books.

www.thehistorypress.co.uk